# Mexico

---

# Tradition, Culture, and Daily Life

## MAJOR NATIONS IN A GLOBAL WORLD

---

# Books in the Series

# Mexico

## Tradition, Culture, and Daily Life

### MAJOR NATIONS IN A GLOBAL WORLD

Michael Centore

Mason Crest

Mason Crest
450 Parkway Drive, Suite D
Broomall, PA 19008
www.masoncrest.com

Printed and bound in the United States of America.

First printing
9 8 7 6 5 4 3 2 1

Series ISBN: 978-1-4222-3339-9
ISBN: 978-1-4222-3348-1
ebook ISBN: 978-1-4222-8588-6

The Library of Congress has cataloged the hardcopy format(s) as follows:

Library of Congress Cataloging-in-Publication Data

Centore, Michael, 1980- author.
  Mexico / by Michael Centore.
   pages cm. -- (Major nations in a global world : tradition, culture, and daily life)
  Summary: Introduces the history, land, culture and economy of Mexico.

  Includes index.
  ISBN 978-1-4222-3348-1 (hardback) -- ISBN 978-1-4222-3339-9 (series) -- ISBN 978-1-4222-8588-6 (ebook)
1.  Mexico--Juvenile literature. 2.  Mexico--Social life and customs--Juvenile literature.  I. Title. II. Series: Major nations in a global world.
  F1208.5.C46 2015
  972--dc23

2015005059

Developed and produced by MTM Publishing, Inc.
        Project Director        Valerie Tomaselli
        Copyeditor              Lee Motteler/Geomap Corp.
        Editorial Coordinator   Andrea St. Aubin

Indexing Services              Andrea Baron, Shearwater Indexing

Art direction and design by Sherry Williams, Oxygen Design Group

# Contents

## KEY ICONS TO LOOK FOR:

**Words to Understand:** These words with their easy-to-understand definitions will increase the reader's understanding of the text, while building vocabulary skills.

**Sidebars:** This boxed material within the main text allows readers to build knowledge, gain insights, explore possibilities, and broaden their perspectives by weaving together additional information to provide realistic and holistic perspectives.

**Research Projects:** Readers are pointed toward areas of further inquiry connected to each chapter. Suggestions are provided for projects that encourage deeper research and analysis.

**Text-Dependent Questions:** These questions send the reader back to the text for more careful attention to the evidence presented there.

**Series Glossary of Key Terms:** This back-of-the book glossary contains terminology used throughout this series. Words found here increase the reader's ability to read and comprehend higher-level books and articles in this field.

The pyramids on the Avenue of the Dead at the famed archaeological site of Teotihuacán in central Mexico, close to the country's present-day capital.

# INTRODUCTION

As the eleventh most populous nation and fourteenth largest by land area, Mexico is a formidable presence on the world's stage. Home to over thirty World Heritage sites, the most in the Americas and the sixth most in the world, the nation's deep and mythic history is clearly of international interest.

Mexico is also a place of stunning natural beauty, with pristine beaches and mountain peaks, rain forests and expansive deserts. At the heart is Mexico City, the political, economic, and cultural capital. Its population of nearly 9 million makes it one of the largest cities in the Western Hemisphere.

Good Friday procession in Jalatlaco, Oaxaca, in southern Mexico.

# WORDS TO UNDERSTAND

**galvanize**: to inspire someone to action.

**indigenous**: native to a region.

**Mesoamerican**: relating to a region extending from central Mexico south to Costa Rica, before the arrival of European influences.

**missionary**: one who goes on a journey to spread a religion.

**waning**: falling gradually from power, prosperity, or influence.

# CHAPTER **1**

# History, Religion, and Tradition

While there is evidence of human habitation in Mexico dating as far back as 11,000 BCE, the first identifiable civilization was the Olmecs. These people lived on the Gulf Coast, near the present-day city of Veracruz, from around 1200 BCE. The Olmecs left few writings, though they did leave a number of artifacts. Through these we know that they had a direct influence on future Mexican civilizations such as the Mayans and the Aztecs. They pioneered many religious practices, stone-carving techniques, and trade and agricultural systems. Their main urban center, San Lorenzo Tenochtitlán, was well advanced for its time.

Olmec culture lasted nearly a thousand years, **waning** around 400 BCE with the abandonment of the city of La Venta. In its wake arose the next major civilization, based around the city of Teotihuacán. Located approximately thirty miles northeast of contemporary Mexico City, construction of Teotihuacán began around 100 BCE and continued consistently for the next three centuries. At its height, the city was one of the largest metropolises in the world, with approximately 150,000 inhabitants. The Pyramids of the Sun and Moon, two of the most famous structures of the **Mesoamerican** world, were also in the city; they remain standing to this day.

## URBAN ADVANCES

Teotihuacán was very advanced in terms of its city planning. Residents lived in one-story apartment complexes that housed anywhere from sixty to one hundred people. Rooms were built around shared patio spaces with altars for communal or family worship. Some were decorated with intricate, colorful murals.

While Teotihuacán was flourishing, the Mayan civilization to the south was spreading across the Yucatán Peninsula and southern Mexico and into Central America. Though the Mayan people had inhabited parts of these areas since approximately 2600 BCE, it was not until 250 CE that the "Classic period" of Mayan civilization emerged. This was a time of great advancement in the fields

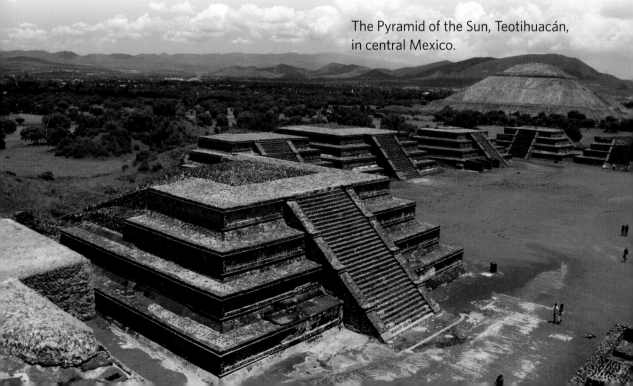

The Pyramid of the Sun, Teotihuacán, in central Mexico.

Toltec warrior sculptures at the central-Mexican archaeological site of Tula.

of mathematics, astronomy, and art. The Maya erected many buildings and monuments, making a network of city-states that united rural and urban populations. By the ninth century, a great part of Mayan civilization mysteriously collapsed; scholars believe this could have been due to environmental factors, such as a drought, or perhaps a foreign invasion or widespread disease.

Two powerful empires followed the Mayans: the Toltec and the Aztec. It is believed that the Toltecs were originally a tribe from north of Teotihuacán. When that city finally fell in the eighth century, they migrated to central Mexico, where they established the capital city of Tula. The Toltec Empire spread outward, often by use of violent force, to claim parts of Mexico, present-day Guatemala, and the Yucatán. After dominating the region for two centuries, the Toltecs were defeated by the Chichimeca, a roving band of tribes from northern Mexico, at the start of the twelfth century.

The Aztecs were a migrant group that came to prominence after founding the city of Tenochtitlán in 1325. In 1428 they formed the "Triple Alliance" with two neighboring cities, Texcoco and Tlacopan. Together the Alliance ruled over central Mexico as the Aztec Empire for the next ninety years. At its peak, the empire

Reproduction of an Aztec mural showing Cortés and La Malinche, a famous woman translator, meeting Montezuma in Tenochtitlán (ca. 1519).

had some 5 million people spread across thirty-eight city-states. All this was to change, however, with the arrival of the Spanish conquistadors in 1519. Led by the blustering Hernán Cortés, the Spanish managed to overthrow Tenochtitlán, ruled at that time by the powerful Montezuma, in only two short years. Cortés was installed as governor, the name of Tenochtitlán was changed to Mexico City, and Spain began a period of colonial rule that would last three hundred years.

Both the physical and social landscapes of Mexico began to change drastically around this time. The Spanish colonialists dismantled many Aztec buildings and erected churches, monasteries, and other structures in their place. They also started mining operations, sending the extracted minerals back to Europe. **Missionaries** arrived from Spain to begin converting the local population to the Roman Catholic faith, an influence still felt today alongside traditions rooted in **indigenous** cultures. Other immigrants came as well, seeking the wealth of the New World. Large plantations called haciendas were set up, run by Spaniards who employed indigenous peoples at low wages. Over time, Spanish became the common language of the country.

By the dawn of the nineteenth century, both landowners who had been born in Mexico and indigenous populations began to express discontent with Spanish rule. They felt the Spanish royalty had too much power, and that they were not adequately represented in the local government. In 1810, a priest named Miguel Hidalgo urged his parish in the central Mexican town of Dolores to fight for independence from Spain. His speech, called the "Cry of Dolores," **galvanized** the people, and soon the movement grew to include inhabitants of many backgrounds. After a long struggle, this united front of Mexicans secured their independence in 1821.

### FREEDOM FIGHTER

Miguel Hidalgo was born in Pénjamo, Mexico, to Spanish parents. After his famous speech, he marched with military commander Ignacio Allende through the neighboring area to rally troops. Though his hope for an independent Mexico was ultimately achieved, it was not without cost: in addition to the many lives lost on both sides during the fight, Hidalgo himself was executed in 1811 by the Spanish authorities.

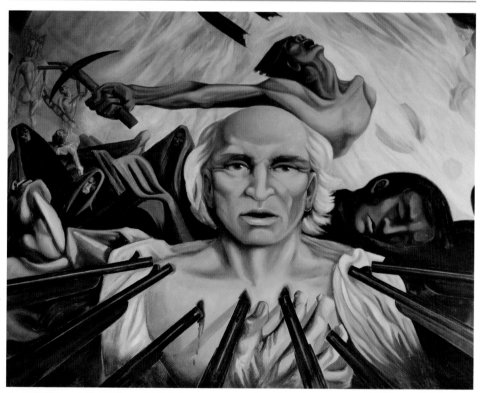

A painting at the Miguel Hidalgo memorial in the government palace of Chihuahua, in northern Mexico.

The transition to independence was a difficult one, with many changes in leadership over the next century. The Mexican-American War further debilitated the country, as over 500,000 square miles (1,295,000 sq km) was ceded to the United States, including much of present-day southwestern and western United States. Unrest continued into the twentieth century, when peasants revolted against the government in 1910 to protest unfair distribution of wealth and power. Two million lives were claimed by the Mexican Revolution, and the end result was rule by a single political party—the Industrial Revolutionary Party—for the remainder of the century. In 2000 Vicente Fox became the first president from outside this party, though its power was restored in 2012 with the election of Enrique Peña Nieto.

## PRESENT PROBLEMS

Modern Mexico faces many challenges of global significance. Emigration of residents to the United States, active drug cartels, and 50 percent of the population living in poverty are a few of the most pressing issues. While foreign investment as a result of globalization has benefited some of the states in the north, the more agrarian, rugged, and rural south has consistently been left behind.

Hand-colored lithograph depicting General Scott's entrance into Mexico during the Mexican-American War, by Adolphe Jean-Baptiste Bayot (1851).

# TEXT-DEPENDENT QUESTIONS

1. In what ways did the early civilizations of Mexico, such as the Olmec and the Maya, contribute to the development of world culture?

2. How did the policies of the Spanish conquistadors change the landscape of Mexico?

3. What were some difficulties of the struggle for Mexican independence from the Spanish, both during and after the transition of power?

# RESEARCH PROJECTS

1. Select one of the thirty-one Mexican states. Research its history, local economy, notable contributions to the Mexican nation, and other points of interest. Write a brief report summarizing your findings.

2. Research one of the key historical figures of the Mexican Revolution (e.g., Porfirio Díaz, Emiliano Zapata, or Pancho Villa). Write a brief biography of this figure, including how he arrived at his political beliefs and his role in the revolution.

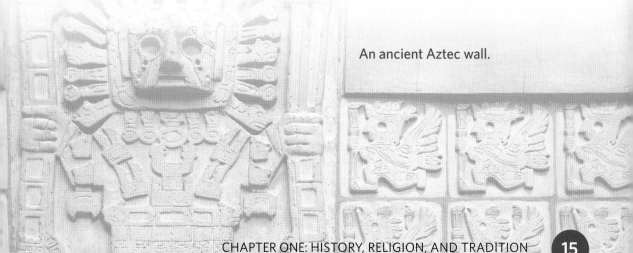

An ancient Aztec wall.

A pilgrimage to the Basilica of Guadalupe at the Plaza of the Americas in Mexico City.

# WORDS TO UNDERSTAND

**homage**: a tribute; a public display of respect for something or someone.

**outstanding**: something that is unpaid or unresolved; continuing to exist.

**patriarchal**: of or relating to male leadership within a particular group or system.

**ragtag**: hastily put together; disorganized.

# CHAPTER 2

# Family and Friends

With one of the lowest divorce rates in the world, Mexico is a place of close-knit relations. Mexican families are traditionally **patriarchal**, with women often confined to childrearing and various domestic tasks, though this is changing as more and more women enter the workforce. Extended families make a point to gather as often as possible, sometimes once a week, forming bonds of trust that are taken very seriously. Friendships are also important sources of emotional support. Friends value each other's internal qualities, such as compassion and spiritual awareness, more than external qualities such as material possessions. It is customary for friends to do favors for one another willingly, without calculating what they are getting in return.

Mexican birthdays are large family affairs. For children, a unique custom is the piñata. This is a papier-mâché construction shaped to resemble an animal. The piñata is filled with candy and small toys, and the young partygoers take turns hitting it with a stick until it breaks and the contents spill onto the floor. They then rush to retrieve the loot.

## THE BIRTHDAY CAKE

At a birthday celebration, the birthday boy or girl is given the honor of having the first bite of cake, though with one rule—no utensils are allowed, and hands must stay behind one's back.

Another occasion that helps bring Mexican families together is the Guelaguetza festival. The word "Guelaguetza" is an ancient Zapotec Indian expression meaning "an exchange of gifts." The festival dates back thousands of years, when indigenous peoples would honor the goddess of corn, Centeotl, in mid-July. During the Spanish colonial period, missionaries merged these ancient rituals with worship of the Virgin of Carmen. Today Guelaguetza is a celebration of indigenous arts, crafts, and dance, with the largest gatherings in Oaxaca City.

A performance of traditional Mexican dances at the Guelaguetza festival in Oaxaca City.

A family tradition unique to Latin American culture is the *quinceañera* (meaning "fifteen years"), a festive celebration of a girl's fifteenth birthday. The history of the *quinceañera* dates back to Aztec rite-of-passage ceremonies, when young women would be ritualistically prepared for their expanded roles in the community. In Mexico, these traditions blended with European customs imported by the Spanish colonialists, such as "coming-out" balls for young women of marrying age.

The *quinceañera* has both religious and social components: in addition to marking the celebrant's transition from girlhood to young womanhood, it is a chance to express thanks to God for granting her a healthy youth. It is also an opportunity for her family to "present" her as an adult capable of taking on new responsibilities. In this

A family celebrates their daughter's *quinceañera*.

way the celebration becomes as much about honoring the efforts of the girl's parents and godparents in raising her as the girl herself.

### AS CLOSE AS PARENTS

The role of the godparent is taken seriously in Mexican culture. In addition to being active participants in the *quinceañera* celebration, godparents act as marital advisors for their godsons or goddaughters. This involves helping plan the wedding, counseling young couples through the early years of marriage, and even helping financially.

In modern-day Mexico, with its large Catholic population, many *quinceañeras* begin with a special mass of thanksgiving. The celebrant wears a formal gown and is accompanied by her *damas*, or maids of honor, and *chambelanes*, or male escorts. Her godparents give her a keepsake such as jewelry or a rosary and may crown her with a tiara. Following the mass, the group repairs to another location for a big party, featuring music, dancing, and an enormous cake. During this reception the father of the young woman will present her with her "last doll," as from this point forward she is expected to put away the toys of her childhood.

In another bow to Catholic tradition, Mexican families gather on January 6 of each year to celebrate the Feast of the Epiphany, or the Day of the Holy Kings. Known as Día de Reyes in Spanish, this feast commemorates the day when the Three Wise Men followed the star of Bethlehem to greet the newborn Jesus with gifts. It comes twelve days after Christmas and is when Mexican children traditionally receive presents. The evening before Día de Reyes, they fill their old shoes with hay for the kings' animals, as well as a "wish list" of things they would like for the coming year. In the morning, the hay is replaced with gifts.

On this day, Mexicans eat a special bread called *rosca de reyes*, or "ring of the kings." This is a sweet pastry formed in the shape of a ring, decorated with dried or candied fruit. According to old European traditions, a lima bean was baked inside the bread to symbolize Jesus's hiding from the wrathful King Herod. Over time, the tradition of the lima bean changed to a plastic reproduction of the infant Jesus. Whoever gets this figurine is considered blessed. He or she must bring it to church on Candlemas (the Feast of the Presentation of Christ) on February 2, as well as host a party that evening with plenty of tamales—a dish made of corn-based dough and meat or vegetable fillings wrapped in leaves and boiled or steamed.

A traditional *rosca de reyes*, or "ring of the kings" pastry.

Two secular holidays are important times for Mexican families and friends to connect. Cinco de Mayo (literally meaning the "fifth of

Dancers perform at the Cinco de Mayo celebration on the grounds of the Washington Monument in Washington D.C., 2010.

May") is actually more popular among Mexican-Americans than Mexicans, though it remains a strong regional custom and symbol of Mexican identity. The celebration dates back to 1861, when the French invaded Mexico in order to collect **outstanding** debts from the government. When they arrived in the city of Puebla in May 1862, they were met by a **ragtag**—and much smaller— Mexican militia, which managed to defeat them. To this day the victory at the Battle of Puebla is celebrated in the state of Puebla with a parade, dancing, and music. In America the holiday has become an unofficial celebration of Mexican culture, as Mexican-Americans pay **homage** to their homeland with concerts and food festivals.

Because of its high profile in America, Cinco de Mayo is often thought to be Mexico's Independence Day. In fact, this is on September 16, the date that the priest Miguel Hidalgo gave a speech in the town of Dolores that motivated his countrymen to rebel against Spanish colonial rule. Today this is a national holiday, and schools, banks, and government buildings are all closed. Families gather to decorate their homes with Mexican flags and colorful flowers. They have parties with large spreads of food, often incorporating the red, white, and green color scheme of the nation's flag. In the evening there are fireworks, and cries of "Viva Mexico!" (or "long live Mexico!") are heard echoing throughout town squares. Much like the American Fourth of July, Mexico's Independence Day is a patriotic and festive occasion.

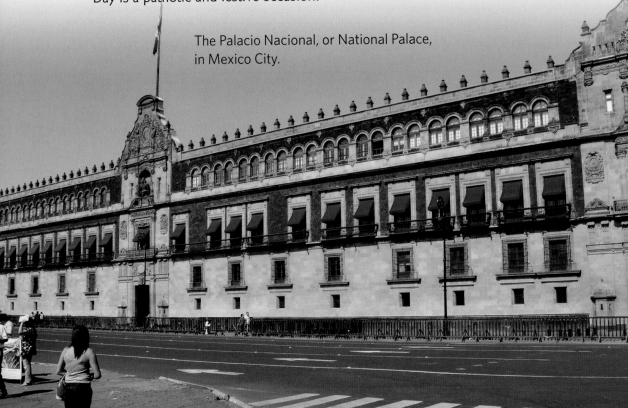

The Palacio Nacional, or National Palace, in Mexico City.

# TEXT-DEPENDENT QUESTIONS

1. What is the social function of the *quinceañera* in a Mexican girl's life?

2. How are the traditions of Día de Reyes different from those of Christmas? How are they similar?

3. What are some important secular holidays in Mexican culture? How do they bring families together?

# RESEARCH PROJECTS

1. Research another life-marking ceremony, such as a baptism, wedding, or school graduation, and how it is celebrated in Mexico. Write a brief report summarizing your findings, being sure to include how the event brings family and friends together.

2. Research how traditional gender roles are changing in twenty-first-century Mexico, especially as more women join the workforce. Write a brief report comparing and contrasting these traditional roles with more contemporary family structures.

A family enjoys ice cream together on a public square.

Chile con carne, a Mexican favorite.

# WORDS TO UNDERSTAND

**appropriate**: to take something and use it for one's own purposes, usually without permission.

**augment**: to enlarge; to make something better by addition.

**concoction**: something that is prepared with many components.

**detonate**: to explode suddenly.

**reconstitute**: to restore something with water.

# CHAPTER 3

# Food and Drink

With its unique mixture of ancient indigenous ingredients that have been cultivated for thousands of years, such as beans and corn, with European-style meats, cheeses, and other foods brought over by the Spanish, Mexican cuisine is one of the most distinct in the world. The country is home to many regional specialties: beef is more widely used in the northern regions, while seafood dominates the coasts. A range of sauces, from mole (made with chocolate and chilies) to guacamole (made with avocados), helps **augment** the flavor of these dishes. The popularity of Mexican cuisine reaches across borders, particularly throughout the southwestern United States.

At the heart of Mexican cooking is the chili pepper. This humble vegetable is used in a wide range of ways—from flavoring dishes to being stuffed with meat or rice and served as a main course. There are hundreds of varieties of chilies. Some are dried and preserved, while others are eaten fresh. Those that are dried may be ground into powder for spice or **reconstituted** and pureed for sauces. There is also a long tradition of smoking chilies in Mesoamerica, a practice that both preserves them and heightens their flavor. One of the most popular of these chilies is the chipotle, which is a smoke-dried jalapeño.

Red chili peppers.

## POPULAR BEANS

Like corn and chilies, beans have been a part of the Mesoamerican diet for thousands of years. The two most popular varieties in Mexico are black beans and pinto beans. Refried beans are made by cooking dried beans, straining them, mashing them into a paste-like consistency, and frying them in lard or oil with garlic. They are often served with rice as a side dish.

Dried pinto beans.

A woman preparing fresh corn tortillas.

Chicken fajitas with cilantro and lime rice, guacamole, and salsa make a delicious Mexican meal—one typical in many Mexican restaurants throughout North America.

A companion to the chili pepper in terms of versatility is corn. A staple crop for millennia, corn remains a valued source of starch in the Mexican diet. It can be grilled on the cob, often served with butter or mayonnaise, lime juice, and a crumbly cheese called *cotija*. A more prevalent use, however, is for making tortillas. This is an ancient recipe that involves removing the kernels from the cob, soaking them in a lime solution to loosen the skins, and grinding them into a paste called masa. The masa is then formed by hand into a thin, circular shape, like a pancake, and placed on a griddle to cook. In the past these griddles were made of clay and placed over an open fire, while today they are often cast iron and heated on stovetops. Modern industrial practices have allowed factories to produce tortillas in large quantities, though many Mexican families still practice making them by hand.

As bread accompanies many of the world's cuisines, so are tortillas present at nearly every Mexican meal. They serve as the base for one of the most recognizable of all Mexican dishes, the taco. No one is quite sure when the taco was added to the Mexican diet. It is possible that an indigenous vegetarian version of the dish existed well before the arrival of the Spanish, perhaps fish or vegetables encased in folded tortilla and garnished with sauces and other items. Later, European influence expanded the variety of fillings with the introduction of beef, chicken, pork, and dairy products.

## TRADITIONAL TORTILLAS

Tortillas can be made of wheat flour as well as corn. A variation on the taco is the burrito, which utilizes a large flour tortilla wrapped completely around a filling. The tortilla is folded in such a way as to make a cylinder-like shape; this makes it easy to eat with one's hands without spilling. The traditional Mexican burrito usually includes meat and refried beans.

The word "taco" originally referred to a "plug." Legend has it that Mexican miners first **appropriated** the word in the eighteenth century to describe the food, as tacos resembled the "plugs" of gunpowder wrapped in paper they used to **detonate** rock. They were quick and easy to prepare and could be eaten while standing up on the job. As a wave of industrialization swept over Mexico in the nineteenth and early twentieth centuries, tacos became a popular "street food" in urban areas. Small stands known as taquerías sprung up to serve workers in need of a fast, inexpensive meal. Today the taquería remains a mainstay of Mexican cities.

A taquería in Morelia, in central Mexico.

Tomatillos, used to make salsa verde, seen at left.

To flavor tacos and other dishes, Mexicans use many types of salsas, or sauces. The most basic of these salsas is *pico de gallo*, a blend of chopped tomatoes, onion, jalapeño or serrano peppers, cilantro, salt, and lime juice. This basic recipe may be varied by roasting the tomatoes and adding garlic to make salsa roja, or "red sauce." Salsa verde, or "green sauce," uses tomatillos, a green tomato-like fruit encircled in a husk, instead of tomatoes to achieve the desired color. Mole poblano is a more involved recipe that includes chocolate, chilies, garlic, peanuts, almonds, and a range of spices; it is often served atop chicken. Guacamole is a mixture of avocados, tomatoes, garlic, onions, and lime juice, which many Mexican cooks prefer to make with a mortar and pestle so as to preserve texture.

Mexican food tends to be rather spicy, which is why it pairs well with *horchata*, one of the country's most popular beverages. Originating in Valencia, Spain, the drink was brought over by the Europeans but is now a favorite throughout Latin America. It is a milky **concoction** made with ground rice blended with hot water and flavored with cinnamon, sugar, and vanilla. In some recipes, almonds, sesame seeds, barley, or tigernuts are also used to give added thickness and flavor. The drink is usually stored in large glass jars with ice and served by ladling it into glasses. Its sweet taste and cool temperature make it an ideal companion for both the warm Mexican climate and the heat of its fiery cuisine.

Desserts are also important in Mexican cuisine. *Pan dulce*, which means "sweet bread," is the all-encompassing term for Mexican pastries. Like many Mexican foods, this dessert bears a European influence, taking inspiration from French baking techniques. *Pan dulce* comes in a whole host of shapes and levels of sweetness. *Conchas* ("shells") are frosted with a butter-and-sugar mixture in a shell-like pattern. *Cuernos* ("horns") are akin to French croissants and have a mild sweetness. *Orejas* ("ears") are so called because they are said to resemble elephants' ears. They are a light, flaky pastry dusted with granulated sugar.

Traditional Mexican sweet breads including *concha*, *pan de muerto*, *pan de reyes*, *cuerno*, and a *churro*.

# TEXT-DEPENDENT QUESTIONS

1. What were some typical food items of indigenous Mexicans/ Mesoamericans, and how did the Mexican/Mesoamerican diet change with the arrival of the Europeans?
2. Why did tacos become such a popular food for the Mexican working class?
3. What are some common ingredients Mexicans use to flavor their food?

# RESEARCH PROJECTS

1. Find a Mexican grocery store in your area or a Mexican food section in your local grocery store. Take notes on the items you find. Write a descriptive report summarizing your experience, researching items you did not recognize.
2. Select two to three of the various regions of Mexico (e.g., Oaxaca or the Yucatán) and research its cuisine. Create a table listing what makes each cuisine unique within Mexico, the ingredients it uses, and how its geography (e.g., its proximity to the ocean or the availability of farmland) influences its food.

Popular Mexican dishes of tacos, chicken tamales, and tortilla chips.

Downtown Mexico City.

# WORDS TO UNDERSTAND

**attest**: to declare something to be true.

**capitalize**: to take advantage of.

**disparity**: a marked difference between things.

**intact**: without damage.

**poised**: to be adequately prepared for something.

# CHAPTER 4

# School, Work, and Industry

Though still plagued by income **disparity** and regional poverty, the economy of Mexico is the fourteenth largest in the world and growing. Many foreign investors, particularly auto manufacturers, have built plants in Mexico to **capitalize** on a large labor force willing to work for lower wages. Other major exports include crude oil and electronic devices such as computers and televisions. While Mexican industry forges ahead into the twenty-first century, traditional handicrafts like pottery, textiles, and metalwork remain sources of income for many residents. Tourism and agriculture help round out the full economic picture of contemporary Mexico.

Lower secondary students participate in class.

Since the Mexican Revolution of 1910, education has been a top priority of the government. The Mexican educational system is divided into several tiers. Preschool covers ages three through five; primary (*primaria*), ages six through eleven; lower secondary (*secundaria*), ages twelve through fourteen; and upper secondary (*preparatoria*), ages fifteen through seventeen. Since 2004 it has been required by law that students complete one year of preschool, and since 2011 upper secondary—akin to American "high school"—has also been compulsory. At the upper secondary level, students can either follow a course for university preparation or one of many technical trades. Over the past thirty years, there has been tremendous growth in the amount of students enrolled in universities. Many of these are private, with low tuitions that make them accessible to those of various backgrounds.

## A HISTORICAL EDUCATION

The National Autonomous University of Mexico is the oldest university in North America. Established in 1551 as the Royal and Pontifical University of Mexico, it was reformed in 1910. In 1929 it was granted total freedom from the government to shape its own curriculum without outside influence. There are over 300,000 students enrolled, ranking among the largest campuses in the world.

There are numerous differences between a typical Mexican student's school day and an American's. The most obvious is that uniforms are required in all levels of Mexican schools. Rather than a letter system on a scale of A through F, Mexican students are graded on a numerical system, with 10 being the highest and 5 being the lowest. Class participation plays a relatively small part of a student's overall evaluation; teachers emphasize recall of information through examinations instead. While students study many of the same subjects as those taught in American schools, such as history, geography, and math, there is a special stress placed on foreign languages from an early age. In some primary schools, bilingual education is offered in English, French, or other languages. Critics **attest** that the Mexican educational system could do better in serving the country's rural populations. Some fear that lack of resources in rural areas leaves students poorly prepared for the challenges of a globalizing economy.

One such example of globalization in Mexico is the growth of the automobile industry. Manufacturers from all over the world have set up factories in Mexico, citing its success in steel production, its network of freight railroads, and a new wave of engineering specialists graduating from Mexican

The National Autonomous University of Mexico in the country's capital.

universities. In 2014 the country became the world's fourth largest exporter of automobiles, and it is **poised** to keep growing throughout the remainder of the decade. Around 100,000 jobs have been created since 2010, leading some to proclaim Mexico as the next Detroit—a reference to the automotive manufacturing capital of the United States.

### CITY OF CARS

One of the major centers of Mexico's growing automotive industry is the city of Aguascalientes. Its population of 1.2 million people is relatively young, which has made for a vibrant workforce. Critics, however, are skeptical of the low wages car companies are paying these workers when compared to those in other countries. They argue that these wages do not provide workers adequate economic mobility.

Another large Mexican industry that continues to expand is that of tourism. Mexico is one of the most visited countries in the world. Travelers flock to its pristine beaches, ancient Mesoamerican sites, and unique religious and cultural festivals. In 2012 alone there were 24 million visitors. This makes tourism the

The beaches in Playacar, on the Yucatán Peninsula in eastern Mexico, are some of the country's most beautiful.

A Zapotec woman sells her handmade rugs in Teotitlan, in southern Mexico.

country's fifth largest source of revenue. The government plans to build more mass-transit systems to help facilitate travel throughout the country over the next few years, hoping to enlarge its place in the Mexican economy even more. Despite violence relating to the illegal drug trade that has affected tourism, there is already noticeable progress, with 14 million visitors arriving in Mexico during the first half of 2014.

## DAY OF THE DEAD

A popular destination for tourists is Oaxaca, Mexico, during Dia de los Muertos, or "Day of the Dead." This is an annual event celebrated between October 31 and November 2. Mexicans in Oaxaca and beyond use this holiday to remember their deceased loved ones by erecting colorful altars, placing flowers at gravesites, and crafting items such as "sugar skulls" and *papel picado*—thin sheets of paper hand cut with elaborate designs.

A large draw for tourists is the experience of Mexico's traditional handicrafts and artisan culture. Each region has its own particular specialty, from Oaxaca's woven tapestries and rugs to the pottery and ceramics of Michoacán. The silversmiths of Taxco in Guerrero are well known for their intricate jewelry, while Santa Clara del Cobre in Michoacán has a high concentration of coppersmiths. These men and women fashion items such as sinks, pitchers, and even bathtubs from copper, often engraving them with intricate

Traditional Day of the Dead altars like this one are colorful and festive.

Huichol yarn painting and beaded crafts for sale.

designs. In the state of Zacatecas, once a center for the mining industry, many of the buildings are adorned with intricate ironwork dating back hundreds of years. Today that tradition continues, as artisans fashion gates and other structures from wrought iron.

A truly independent ethnic group in Mexico is the Huichol people, who live in the Sierra Madre Occidental mountain range. They escaped the influence of the Europeans during the colonial era and consequently have preserved many of their artistic and cultural traditions **intact**. They are known for their colorful beadwork, which they use to adorn everything from household items to religious objects. These one-of-a-kind works of art have attracted popularity outside of Mexico and have become a stable source of income for many Huichol.

## PAINTING WITH YARN

The Huichol also work in a medium known as "yarn painting." This involves coating a wooden surface with melted beeswax, then embedding strands of colored yarn into the wax to create images and patterns. Many of these images reflect the spiritual dimension of the Huichol, depicting religious visions and iconography in bold colors.

# TEXT-DEPENDENT QUESTIONS

1. What are some of the main components of the Mexican economy?
2. How has the automotive industry changed in Mexico over the past several decades?
3. Cite examples of traditional arts and crafts that have remained part of Mexican culture.

# RESEARCH PROJECTS

1. Research an area of Mexico that is a popular tourist destination. Write a brief report summarizing the location, what it offers travelers, and how it may have changed over time.
2. Research a traditional Mexican handicraft not covered in this chapter. Write a brief summary of its history within Mexican culture, where and how it is practiced, and what its decorative and/or practical uses are.

A woman sells handcrafted black pottery at the market in Tlacolula, in southern Mexico.

Giovanni Dos Santos of Mexico in a match against Chile.

# WORDS TO UNDERSTAND

**commemoration**: the act of remembering someone or something, usually with a ceremony or event.

**esteemed**: held in high regard.

**purveyor**: one who sells a certain good.

**repertoire**: the pieces of music that a group or individual is prepared to perform.

**tempestuous**: volatile, stormy, emotionally charged.

# CHAPTER 5

# Arts and Entertainment

Mexicans are a very festive, fun-loving people. They value their families, friends, and fellow citizens, always making time to enjoy the moment with others. Various annual celebrations, such as the events of Semana Santa (Holy Week) leading up to Easter or the ancestral **commemorations** of Dia de los Muertos (Day of the Dead) in the autumn, demonstrate Mexicans' commitment to honoring their history and each other. This vivacious spirit is matched in the Mexican passion for sports and is also reflected in the country's art and music.

A Mexican *charro* participates in a *charreada* competition near San Antonio, Texas, across Mexico's northern border.

### HOLY WEEK

Semana Santa, or Holy Week, is one of the most important holidays on the Mexican calendar. It takes place during the week leading up to Easter. Ways of marking the occasion differ from village to village, though many enact a "Passion Play"—a depiction of the last hours in the life of Christ, with villagers taking on the different roles.

In addition to soccer and other contemporary sports, Mexicans bring their passion and flare to *charreada*. Similar to rodeo and perhaps more art than sport, *charreada* has its roots in the cowboy culture of the Mexican hacienda, where ranching and raising cattle was a way of life. *Charreada* involves a competition between teams of *charros*, those who perform stunts and feats of horseback riding. There are nine events in all. The competition opens with a colorful procession as participants parade into an arena during the opening ceremonies. Mexican-Americans north of the border also hold these festive games and sometimes compete for the national championship in Mexico.

The Mexican penchant for festive celebrations is also seen the "Night of the Radishes," a carnival that takes place in the *zócalo*, or central square, of Oaxaca City every December 23. At this event, artisans carve giant radishes and other root vegetables into the shapes of humans, animals, buildings, religious scenes, and anything else they can envision. The festival lasts no more than a few hours, which is about the average lifespan of the carvings. At the end of the evening, judges select their favorites and award prizes to the victors. The winner gets a cash prize as well as his or her picture splashed across the pages of the local newspaper.

The festival draws thousands of residents and tourists alike, and special crops of radishes are grown separately for the participants. Parades, fireworks, craft vendors, and local food **purveyors** are some of the other types of entertainment on hand as everyone gets into the Christmas spirit.

It is clear from festivals such as Night of the Radishes that art plays a central role in the social and cultural life of Mexico. Among the most **esteemed** of all Mexican artists is the painter Frida Kahlo. She was born in 1907 in Coyoacán, then a small suburb outside of Mexico City, to a German father and Mexican mother. Her young life was marked by two events that permanently altered her health: at age six, she contracted polio, leaving one of her legs thinner and weaker than the

other; and at age eighteen, she was involved in a severe bus accident and sustained injuries throughout her body. The accident would impair her ability to have children, and over the course of her life she would require over thirty operations.

An elaborate sculpture done for the Night of the Radishes carnival in 2014.

A street view of Frida Kahlo's La Casa Azul, or The Blue House.

## THE BLUE HOUSE

The birthplace of Frida Kahlo is known as La Casa Azul, or "The Blue House." The house gets its name from its striking cobalt-blue walls. Today it has been turned into a museum, containing original canvases, household objects, and other memorabilia from Kahlo's life. It is one of the most popular museums in all of Mexico City.

The physical and psychological stress of her childhood, as well as her **tempestuous** marriage to fellow Mexican painter Diego Rivera, became the raw material for her paintings. Kahlo is most famous for her self-portraits, which use a rich symbolic vocabulary to depict her interior life and struggles. Their bright color palettes and primitive "folk-art" style are reminiscent of indigenous Mexican painting. Though some critics called her work "surreal," meaning that it represented the dreamlike world of the imagination, Kahlo always insisted that she was a realist and that her paintings were her true autobiography. She died in 1954 at age forty-seven. Since then her popularity has continued to grow. In addition to being one of Mexico's great cultural figures, she is now seen as an early feminist icon who helped blaze the trail for independent female artists worldwide.

*Exploitation of Mexico by Spanish Conquistadors* (1929-1945) by Diego Rivera is one of many murals he painted in Mexico's National Palace.

*Frieda and Diego Rivera* (1931) by Frida Kahlo.

## A PROMINENT MURALIST

Frida Kahlo's husband, Diego Rivera, was a towering artist in his own right. Born in 1886, Rivera rose to prominence as a muralist in the 1920s. These massive paintings, done on the walls of public spaces, depicted events of Mexican history. In the 1930s he completed murals in several American locations, including the Detroit Institute of the Arts, and his work began to address the plight of the working class.

Along with the visual arts, music is a vital component of Mexican life. Weddings, *quinceañeras*, and other large gatherings often feature an ensemble playing a traditional folk music of Mexico known as mariachi. The word can mean both the type of music and the musicians themselves. The songs in the mariachi **repertoire** deal with elemental human themes—love, death, revolution—yet their spirited delivery encourages people to dance.

Mariachi was developed in the nineteenth century in the state of Jalisco. The earliest mariachi players were itinerant laborers who traveled from farm to farm, usually playing stringed instruments. By the end of the century, these musicians had incorporated more European-style elements into their performances, such as waltzes. They began to play shows in theaters and concert halls. The mariachi lineup evolved to feature violins, trumpets, and a special five-string guitar called a *vihuela*. By the early twentieth century, performers began to wear "*charro*" suits: a traditional Mexican horseman's uniform, often adorned with silver studs and accompanied by a large sombrero.

## MUSIC FROM THE RANCH

Closely related to mariachi music is *ranchera*, a style of folk music often performed by a lone singer and a guitar. The word *ranchera* comes from "ranch," as this music was originally played on the rural ranches of the Mexican countryside. With its earthy songs of love, country, and the natural world, *ranchera* was especially popular during the Mexican Revolution.

Today mariachi continues to thrive both in and outside of Mexico. There are active groups in Europe, Latin America, and the United States. The International Mariachi Festival of Guadalajara is an annual event that brings together the world's top mariachi performers. The music will forever be associated with its Mexican heritage, however. In restaurants and public squares, at birthdays and weddings, Mexican mariachi combos ply their craft daily to entertain people of all walks of life.

Mariachi musicians playing a *vihuela* and a trumpet.

# TEXT-DEPENDENT QUESTIONS

1. How do celebrations such as the Night of the Radishes honor Mexico's agricultural heritage?

2. What were some qualities of Frida Kahlo's work that link it to the tradition of Mexican indigenous art?

3. Why might mariachi music have such broad appeal, both in and outside of Mexico?

# RESEARCH PROJECTS

1. Research another site of Mexican arts and entertainment, such as the Palacio de Bellas Artes in Mexico City, or another important Mexican festival, such as the Feast of Our Lady of Guadalupe. Create a slide show illustrating its history, significance, and the entertainment it provides and/or how it is celebrated. Use captions to explain the images and fill in details.

2. Research a popular Mexican musician who worked (or is currently working) in the field of mariachi or *ranchera*. Write a brief biography of his or her life, including his or her contributions to Mexico's musical history.

The Palacio de Bellas Artes, or Palace of Fine Arts, in Mexico City.

Ancient ruins of Palenque,
in southern Mexico.

# WORDS TO UNDERSTAND

**acclimate**: to adapt oneself to a new environment or set of conditions.

**façade**: the face of a building.

**huaraches**: sandals made of interwoven leather strips.

**plumed**: adorned with or covered by feathers.

**unsullied**: not tarnished or damaged.

# CHAPTER 6

# Cities, Towns, and the Countryside

Mexico is a land of diverse physical terrain. Its miles of coastline on both the Pacific Ocean and the Gulf of Mexico attract thousands of beachgoers each year. The majestic Copper Canyon in Chihuahua is even larger than the Grand Canyon in Arizona. Desert regions such as the Sonoran and Chihuahuan are harsh climates for humans, yet biologically diverse. Further south, the Lacandon Jungle in Chiapas is home to one of the largest rain forests in North America. Mexico's cities, towns, and villages are vibrant social landscapes, and various regional differences—from food to music—help preserve an authentic sense of culture.

The Urique River in Copper Canyon, Chihuahua, Mexico.

In the Copper Canyon lives one of Mexico's more mysterious Native American groups, the Tarahumara. Also known as the Rarámuri, the Tarahumara are originally from the Chihuahua region in northern Mexico. When the Spanish arrived in the sixteenth century, the group fled to the remote regions of Copper Canyon and the Sierra Madre Occidental mountains. In this way they were able to preserve their traditions and way of life **unsullied** by European influence. They also steered clear of such European-imported diseases as smallpox. The Tarahumara faced another wave of invasion when the lands they occupied became centers for mining. This forced them to escape deeper into the Mexican wilderness, where they continued to grow beans and corn and raise livestock for subsistence.

## THE LACANDON JUNGLE

Stretching from Chiapas to Guatemala and into the Yucatán Penninsula, the Lacandon Jungle is a very fertile area, with 1,500 species of trees alone. The Montes Azules Biosphere Reserve is located within the jungle, protecting over 150,000 acres (607 sq km) of lagoons, rivers (including the Usumacinta, one of the longest in Mexico), and endangered species. The Lacandon Jungle is also known for its many Mayan archaeological sites.

What the Tarahumara are most known for, however, is their uncanny athletic ability, particularly in the field of long-distance running. Over the centuries, they came to depend on running as both a form of transport and a way to hunt animals. Even today it is not uncommon for the Tarahumara to run distances of over 100 miles (161 km) at once. While there are still practical components to their running, there are recreational aspects as well. For instance, the contest of "foot throwing" is a long, sometimes multiday relay race in which teams of runners advance a wooden ball toward the finish line. The runners wear sandals or **huaraches** and brightly colored tunics. Today there are somewhere between 50,000 and 75,000 Tarahumara in the vicinity of Copper Canyon.

Between the Mexican states of Veracruz and Puebla sits the third highest peak in North America, Pico de Orizaba. At 18,491 feet (5,636 m), only Mount McKinley (Denali) in Alaska and Mount Logan in Canada are higher. Pico de Orizaba is actually a volcano, which makes it the highest active volcano in North America. It was formed over a million years ago by volcanic activity, and most recently erupted in the nineteenth century.

### ISOLATED LIVING

Guadalupe Island, located 150 miles (241 km) west of the Baja Peninsula in the Pacific Ocean, is a rugged, volcanic landscape with a scant population of thirty families. They make their livelihood fishing for abalone and lobsters. Isolated in small fishing camps, they are dependent on generators for power and receive special deliveries of fresh water from military ships.

The Pico de Orizaba volcano, the highest mountain in Mexico, located in the south of the country.

The garden of Castillo de Chapultepec, in Mexico City.

Pico de Orizaba had great significance for precolonial cultures. The Aztecs, for instance, believed that sacred fire from the volcano destroyed Quetzal-coatl—a deity in the form of a **plumed** serpent. The Aztec name for the peak was Citlaltépetl, a Nahuatl word that means "star mountain." Its current name comes from the Orizaba Valley, which is visible from the summit. Nine glaciers, mostly on the colder north and northwest faces, cap the mountain.

In 1936 the area around Pico de Orizaba was set aside as a preserved park. Besides being an indomitable physical landmark, the mountain is a popular destination for climbers worldwide. Small communities around the base support a modest tourist economy by supplying guides and coordinating summiting trips for visitors. While the route to the top is rather direct, climbers must have experience with icy conditions and be able to **acclimate** to high altitudes.

## A PARK WITH HISTORY

Chapultepec Park in Mexico City is the largest urban park in the world. Its main geographical feature is Chapultepec Hill, which the Aztecs adorned with an altar. In the eighteenth century, a palace was built atop the hill as a home for Spanish colonial governors and later, until 1939, for the Mexican president. Today it is home to the National Museum of History.

Far removed from the isolated tribes of the Tarahumara and the high, wild terrain of Pico de Orizaba are the urban centers of Mexico. Of these, Mexico City is by far the largest. Here are located some of Mexico's most stunning buildings, from the ornate Metropolitan Cathedral to the sprawling Palacio Nacional. The latter has been the seat of the Mexican government since the days of the Aztecs. The Palacio de Bellas Artes (Palace of Fine Arts) is a beautiful fusion of architectural styles that blend traditional and modern elements. Completed in 1934, it remains a working theater, hosting plays, ballet, and opera performances.

In the twenty-first century, Mexico City continues to build on its rich architectural heritage. One striking example is the Museo Soumaya (Soumaya Museum) in the New Polanco neighborhood. Designed by Mexican architect Fernando Romero, the structure resembles an organic life form, with **façades** that curve in from the base and expand outward toward the sky. Each surface is covered with aluminum panels—16,000 in all—that scatter reflected sunlight in all directions. On the top floor of the museum, a great skylight illuminates the sculpture garden.

An aerial view of Mexico City and the Palace of Fine Arts, lower right.

### TUNNEL TRAVEL

When the city of Guanajuato, in a narrow valley in southern Mexico, suffered from excessive flooding in the late 1700s, construction began on a series of tunnels to help divert the water. In the 1960s, the local government paved the tunnels with cobblestones, lighted them, and used them as roads for vehicular traffic. Today pedestrians and drivers utilize this vast subterranean network to navigate the city.

Romero will have yet another opportunity to transform the landscape of Mexico City when he partners with British architect Norman Foster to design a new international airport. The futuristic-looking building will be the most advanced airport design in the world upon its completion. It will utilize environmentally sustainable methods of construction, will be equipped to collect, store, and reuse rainwater, and will employ the latest methods of solar technology to generate power. The airport is scheduled to open in 2018.

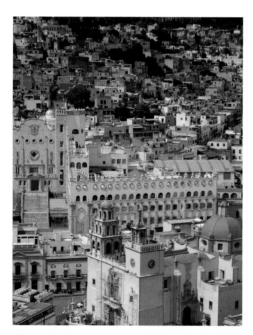

The colorful buildings of Guanajuato, in central Mexico, along with a street view on the right.

A typical street in Guanajuato, Mexico.

# TEXT-DEPENDENT QUESTIONS

1. How have the Tarahumara managed to remain so independent throughout the centuries?
2. In what ways has Pico de Orizaba contributed to the cultural and economic life of the region of Puebla-Veracruz?
3. How has Mexico City both preserved and furthered its great architectural tradition?

# RESEARCH PROJECTS

1. Research one of the main agricultural crops of Mexico, such as corn, avocados, agave, or chili peppers. Write a brief report explaining the area in which the crop is grown, how it is harvested, how it impacts surrounding towns or villages, and its cultural significance.
2. Research one of Mexico's many coastal towns on either the Gulf of Mexico or the Pacific Ocean. Write a brief report summarizing your findings, including the history of the town and how it contributes to Mexican culture. Pay special attention to how the sea influences the life of the people.

Isla Mujeres in Cancún, on the Yucatán Peninsula in eastern Mexico.

# FURTHER RESEARCH

**Online**

The Central Intelligence Agency's World Fact Book on Mexico provides up-to-date statistics, a short history, and maps: https://www.cia.gov/library/publications/the-world-factbook/geos/mx.html.

Find Mexico's government website at http://en.presidencia.gob.mx.

Learn more about Mexican food by visiting http://www.differentworld.com/mexico/food.htm.

Learn more about Mexican culture by visiting http://www.everyculture.com/Ma-Ni/Mexico.html and http://www.kwintessential.co.uk/resources/global-etiquette/mexico-country-profile.html.

Learn more about Mexico's history and its thirty-two states: http://www.history.com/topics/mexico.

**Books**

Bayless, Rick. *Authentic Mexican: Regional Cooking from the Heart of Mexico.* New York: William Marrow Cookbooks, 2007.

Franz, Carl. *The People's Guide to Mexico.* Berkeley: Avalon Travel, 2012.

Mavor, Guy. *Mexico: Culture Smart!* London: Kuperard, 2006.

Lonely Planet. *Mexico: Travel Guide.* Victoria, AU: Lonely Planet, 2014.

NOTE TO EDUCATORS: This book contains both imperial and metric measurements as well as references to global practices and trends in an effort to encourage the student to gain a worldly perspective. We, as publishers, feel it's our role to give young adults the tools they need to thrive in a global society.

# SERIES GLOSSARY

**ancestral**: relating to ancestors, or relatives who have lived in the past.

**archaeologist**: a scientist that investigates past societies by digging in the earth to examine their remains.

**artisanal**: describing something produced on a small scale, usually handmade by skilled craftspeople.

**colony**: a settlement in another country or place that is controlled by a "home" country.

**commonwealth**: an association of sovereign nations unified by common cultural, political, and economic interests and traits.

**communism**: a social and economic philosophy characterized by a classless society and the absence of private property.

**continent**: any of the seven large land masses that constitute most of the dry land on the surface of the earth.

**cosmopolitan**: worldly; showing the influence of many cultures.

**culinary**: relating to the kitchen, cookery, and style of eating.

**cultivated**: planted and harvested for food, as opposed to the growth of plants in the wild.

**currency**: a system of money.

**demographics**: the study of population trends.

**denomination**: a religious grouping within a faith that has its own organization.

**dynasty**: a ruling family that extends across generations, usually in an autocratic form of government, such as a monarchy.

**ecosystems**: environments where interdependent organisms live.

**endemic**: native, or not introduced, to a particular region, and not naturally found in other areas.

**exile**: absence from one's country or home, usually enforced by a government for political or religious reasons.

**feudal**: a system of economic, political, or social organization in which poor landholders are subservient to wealthy landlords; used mostly in relation to the Middle Ages.

**globalization**: the processes relating to increasing international exchange that have resulted in faster, easier connections across the world.

**gross national product**: the measure of all the products and services a country produces in a year.

**heritage**: tradition and history.

**homogenization**: the process of blending elements together, sometimes resulting in a less interesting mixture.

**iconic**: relating to something that has become an emblem or symbol.

**idiom**: the language particular to a community or class; usually refers to regular, "everyday" speech.

**immigrants**: people who move to and settle in a new country.

**indigenous**: originating in and naturally from a particular region or country.

**industrialization**: the process by which a country changes from a farming society to one that is based on industry and manufacturing.

#  SERIES GLOSSARY

**integration**: the process of opening up a place, community, or organization to all types of people.

**kinship**: web of social relationships that have a common origin derived from ancestors and family.

**literacy rate**: the percentage of people who can read and write.

**matriarchal**: of or relating to female leadership within a particular group or system.

**migrant**: a person who moves from one place to another, usually for reasons of employment or economic improvement.

**militarized**: warlike or military in character and thought.

**missionary**: one who goes on a journey to spread a religion.

**monopoly**: a situation where one company or state controls the market for an industry or product.

**natural resources**: naturally occurring materials, such as oil, coal, and gold, that can be used by people.

**nomadic**: describing a way of life in which people move, usually seasonally, from place to place in search of food, water, and pastureland.

**nomadic**: relating to people who have no fixed residence and move from place to place.

**parliament**: a body of government responsible for enacting laws.

**patriarchal**: of or relating to male leadership within a particular group or system.

**patrilineal**: relating to the relationship based on the father or the descendants through the male line.

**polygamy**: the practice of having more than one spouse.

**provincial**: belonging to a province or region outside of the main cities of a country.

**racism**: prejudice or animosity against people belonging to other races.

**ritualize**: to mark or perform with specific behaviors or observances.

**sector**: part or aspect of something, especially of a country's or region's economy.

**secular**: relating to worldly concerns; not religious.

**societal**: relating to the order, structure, or functioning of society or community.

**socioeconomic**: relating to social and economic factors, such as education and income, often used when discussing how classes, or levels of society, are formed.

**statecraft**: the ideas about and methods of running a government.

**traditional**: relating to something that is based on old historical ways of doing things.

**urban sprawl**: the uncontrolled expansion of urban areas away from the center of the city into remote, outlying areas.

**urbanization**: the increasing movement of people from rural areas to cities, usually in search of economic improvement, and the conditions resulting this migration.

# INDEX

# INDEX

# INDEX

# INDEX

# PHOTO CREDITS

# ABOUT THE AUTHOR

**Michael Centore** is a writer and editor. He has helped produce many titles, including memoirs, cookbooks, and educational materials, among others, for a variety of publishers. He has experience in several facets of book production, from photo research to fact checking. His poetry and essays have appeared in *Crux*, *Tight*, *Mockingbird*, and other print- and web-based publications. Prior to his involvement in publishing, he worked as a stone mason, art handler, and housepainter. He was born in Hartford, Connecticut, and lives in Brooklyn, New York.